THE JOY OF BEING A LECTOR

Mitch Finley

Foreword by
Rev. Joseph M. Champlin

Resurrection Press
An Imprint of
CATHOLIC BOOK PUBLISHING CORP.
Totowa • New Jersey

Dedication

THIS BOOK is for John Leonardi and Emilie Cerar for whom publishing is a ministry of the word and an affair of the heart. It's an honor to write for two such dedicated and gifted people.

Nihil Obstat
REV. JOHN M. STEINER, VG
Censor Librorum
Spokane, Washington

Imprimatur
✠ MOST REVEREND WILLIAM S. SKYLSTAD
Bishop of Spokane
Spokane, Washington

First published in February, 2000 by

Catholic Book Publishing/Resurrection Press
77 West End Road
Totowa, NJ 07512

ISBN 978-1-878718-57-0 Library of Congress Catalog Number 99-75981

Unless otherwise noted, all quotations from Scripture are from the New American Bible with Revised New Testament, copyright © 1986 by the Confraternity of Christian Doctrine. All rights reserved.

Cover design by John Murello. Printed in Canada.

4   5   6   7   8   9   10   11   12   13   14   15

CONTENTS

WHETHER COMMISSIONED READERS OR NOT, [lectors] should be competent and carefully prepared for the task. This preparation should be primarily spiritual, but technical training is also needed. The spiritual preparation presupposes at least a biblical and liturgical formation. The biblical formation should aim at imparting an understanding of the readings in their context and a grasp, by faith, of the central point of the revealed message. The liturgical formation should give some understanding of the meaning and structure of the liturgy of the word and the relationship between the liturgy of the word and the liturgy of the eucharist. The technical training should teach how to read in public, with and without an amplification system.

— General Instruction
for the Lectionary (no. 55)

Foreword

FOR MOST ROMAN CATHOLICS, receiving Holy Communion is the peak religious experience of their lives, whether that occurs on a regular or only occasional basis. This action bonds them in a unique way for a few minutes with a group of other believers and with the Lord.

Moreover, the short, silent interval which follows the return to their seats has an intensely personal quality to it. As a presiding priest gazing at that time over many bowed heads and closed eyes, I marvel at the diverse, intimate and hidden conversations which must be going on in those numerous minds and hearts.

Something very similar, but less evident occurs when lectors proclaim and priests or deacons preach the Word. The assembled people hear the message together as a faith community, but each person receives the message in a very individualized fashion.

When someone comments on a homily after Mass, I am quite intrigued by what idea or illustration particularly touched them. The concept may have been a minor point or even unrelated to the main message but, interpreted personally, nevertheless impacts the listener to a significant degree.

This concept — the individualized and personal reception of the Eucharist and the Word — is a key insight of Mitch Finley's wonderful little book.

It reminds lectors of how their proclaimed words are touching many hearts in varied ways.

However, *The Joy of Being a Lector* underscores another critical truth about proclaiming the Scriptures. Lectors are not doing this on their own. The author cites a pivotal paragraph from the *Constitution on the Sacred Liturgy*, No. 7, which describes the multiple manner in which Christ is present in the Church. Included among these, the passage states, is the presence of Jesus in the biblical readings, so that when the Scriptures are proclaimed, Christ is proclaimed. This remarkable notion should serve both as a challenge and an encouragement for lectors.

There are, in addition, many other elements about Finley's book which make it recommended reading for all who fulfill this ministry.

• It is short. Today's busy volunteer readers would probably find a massive tome on the subject off-putting.

• It is eminently readable.

• It is rich in theology, history and liturgy, with sections featuring each of these disciplines.

• It is practical, full of useful suggestions on how to be a better lector.

My experience with lectors over the past forty years has been that, while proclaiming the Word is a much more difficult and demanding task than serving as a Eucharistic minister, readers seem less liable to attend training workshops or study helpful manuals. I hope *The Joy of Being a Lector* will alter that trend and enjoy the success of his earlier, but similar book, *The Joy of Being a Eucharistic Minister*.

Father Joseph Champlin, Rector
Cathedral of the Immaculate Conception
Syracuse, New York

WELCOME TO THE MINISTRY
OF LECTOR

THE WORD "LECTOR" comes from the Latin, *legere*, "to read." A lector is someone who reads. More specifically, a lector is one who reads aloud in the context of a church service for the benefit of the congregation. Even more specifically, for Catholics a lector is one who reads aloud from the Scriptures in the context of that part of the Mass called the Liturgy of the Word. It is important to note that the ministry of lector is an authentic and official *ministry* of the Catholic Church. It not just a "volunteer activity."

> Pope Paul VI's apostolic letter *Ministeria Quaedam* (1972) set aside the Council of Trent's notion that all ministries below priesthood are simply steps toward the priesthood, and restored lay ministries to the Latin Church, to be conferred not by ordination but by installation. The apostolic letter established two lay ministries, those of lector and acolyte. . .[1]

Many Catholics tend to think of the Liturgy of the Word as secondary. We tend to view it as a liturgical preface to the Real Thing, namely the Liturgy of the Eucharist, where the bread and wine become the body and blood — or whole person — of the risen Christ.[2] Protestant worship services are often limited to a Liturgy of the Word, therefore many Catholics tend to think of "all that Bible stuff" as "Protestant." We cling fiercely to the eucharist itself as the most important part of the liturgy. Sure, the readings from Scripture are fine, and we'll hike a country mile to hear a gifted homilist. But when push comes to shove, if we had to choose we would take the Liturgy of the Eucharist over the Liturgy of the Word every time. Indeed, many weekday Masses include little or no homily, and most Catholics don't complain.

Unfortunately, to cling to this attitude is to miss out. Big time. The Mass has two parts for a reason, and the sooner we begin to appreciate this, the sooner we will benefit from the wisdom of the Church in giving us both the Liturgy of the Word and the Liturgy of the Eucharist. Some Catholics may think of the Liturgy of the Word as less important, but even a quick glance at various Protestant traditions reveals the power of the Scriptures. Even Protestant communities that have been strictly communities of the word for centuries have been able to maintain a lively communion with the risen Christ through their love for the word of God in Holy Scripture. The Scriptures have a power to shape and nourish a community of faith that we Catholics sometimes overlook.

Catholics believe that Protestant communities miss a great deal by not having the eucharist and the eucharistic real presence. But Catholic communities miss a great deal by not appreciating the Liturgy of the Word as much as they could. Even with all the encouragement the Church, since Vatican Council II in the mid-1960s, has given to intimacy with and knowledge of the scriptures, many — perhaps most — Catholics still have a less than satisfactory knowledge of the Bible.

As a lector, or as someone planning to become a lector, knowledge of and familiarity with the scriptures is a top priority. To read aloud from the scriptures with little understanding of what you are reading is like getting behind the wheel of a car not knowing where the ignition is. Does this mean you need to become an expert on the Bible? Of course not, no more than driving a car requires you to become an expert mechanic. Does it mean that you need to become more knowledgeable about the Bible and cultivate a deeper intimacy with the scriptures than you had before? You're darn tootin' it does.

Beginning with this little book, as a lector you are called to become better informed about the scriptures than you were before. An important part of this book offers a thumbnail introduction to Scripture. You are called to spend more time learning about, reading, and praying with the scriptures. Before you begin to wonder where you will find the time, however, keep one thing in mind. You can count on this: the more time you spend with the

Scriptures, the more time you will want to spend with the Scriptures. It's habit forming, in the best sense of the term.

Why is it so important to be well informed about the Bible? In a nutshell, we Catholics believe that divine revelation comes to us in two forms, and both need to be present if revelation is to be complete. We believe that both Scripture and Sacred Tradition carry the living word of God.

Sacred Tradition — meaning not mere "customs" and "traditions," but all the non-scriptural ways God speaks to us in the church — we generally have no trouble understanding. Scripture, however, we tend to overlook, primarily because Protestants have emphasized it for so long, and we don't want to "act like Protestants." Since Vatican II, however, the time has come for Catholics to act more like Protestants, at least in this regard. At the same time, it has also come time for Protestants to "act more like Catholics," and this has in fact happened as we witness a renewed interest in liturgy among mainline Protestant churches since Vatican II.

It's not our task to tell Protestants what to do, however. It is our task to give the Scriptures more attention and become better informed about the Scriptures, while at the same time clinging to our love for the eucharist. Indeed, the closer we draw to the word of God in Scripture, the closer we will find ourselves growing to the risen Christ who gives his whole risen self to us in the eucharist, "body and blood, soul and divinity."

Welcome, then, to the ministry of lector. As you increase your understanding of this ministry, and how to carry it out well, you will discover that you become stronger in your faith in other ways, too. You will discover that a lector is far more than someone who simply stands up and reads aloud from the Lectionary. Much, much more than that. . .

1. Richard P. McBrien, *Catholicism*, New Edition (San Francisco: HarperSanFrancisco, 1994), 771.
2. See Mitch Finley, *The Joy of Being a Eucharistic Minister* (Mineola, NY: Resurrection Press, 1998).

PART I

THE SPIRITUALITY OF THE LECTOR

"SPIRITUALITY" is a tricky word, a word used any number of ways depending on who uses it, and where, and when, and why. There are many kinds of "spirituality" out there. For our purposes, we want to discuss Christian spirituality and how it makes you who you are. Then we will look at some unique characteristics of Christian spirituality for the ministry of lector.

Pigs with Haloes and Wings

It may be helpful if we sneak up on the topic of spirituality from an unexpected direction, prepared for surprises. Ready? Attend to some words from author Frederick Buechner:

> Any Christian who is not a hero, Léon Bloy wrote, is a pig. . . From time to time I find a kind of heroism momentarily possible — a seeing, doing, telling of Christly truth — but most of the time I am indistinguishable from the rest of the herd that jostles and snuffles at the great trough of life.[1]

You and I inhabit a culture that drives a wedge between religion and spirituality and the rest of life. Each of us is a part-time worker at whatever work we do. Religious people, most of them anyway, also work parttime at being religious. And each of us, yes, is a parttime. . ."pig." Buechner borrows this metaphor from early twentieth-century French Catholic poet Léon Bloy, and it is mighty harsh, this metaphor. But it has the ring of truth, too. Christians living in a secular culture, much of the time are "indistinguishable from the rest of the herd that jostles and snuffles at the great trough of life."

Greetings, fellow pigs. Oink, oink.

This is not all there is to say, of course. Definitely not. For what is most true about you is what is deepest in your heart. Even if, necessarily, you spend much of your time jostling and snuffling at the great trough of life, what matters most is what is deepest in your heart. What matters most is what gets you out of bed in the morning, day after day, to live your gloriously ordinary life. What matters most is *why* you go to work, *why* you cherish your faith, and *why* you keep trying to live your life in union with the risen Christ and in his Holy Spirit. *This* is what spirituality is about. This is what spirituality *means*.

Your spirituality, oh Christian, comes from how you face, each day, the holy mysteries three: the holy mystery of the day ahead of you, the holy mystery of your own self, and the holy mystery of God's unconditional loving presence in you and in everything and everyone you encounter. How do you do this? What are your strategies, plans, schedules, customs and habits? Your response to this question describes your spirituality, and each one of us gives a unique response. Each one of us has a special spirituality, unique ways we live with and in the holy mysteries. *With* and *in* the holy mysteries.

In other words, Léon Bloy's French poetic crack about our porcine ways is true. We can jostle and snuffle with the best of them at the great trough of life. But this observation just skims the surface. Only the surface, *mon ami*. For in the secret recesses of your heart, where you are most who you are, your true self, you cling with all your might to your Christian faith, to your loving intimacy with the risen Lord. It's true for you, it's true for me, and it's true for countless people the world over.

Not only this, but in our better moments because of our spirituality even our jostling and snuffling — our ordinary daily efforts, the practical ways we care for one another, the persistence with which we earn a living, try to be faithful to our promises, and try to trust in God's love — becomes holy. Yes! We jostle and snuffle with all the other, um, pigs. But with this difference. The eyes of faith see above our heads saintly haloes. Slightly tarnished, but haloes all the same. And sprouting from our backs are the beginnings of feathery wings. Pigs with tarnished haloes starting to sprout the wings of angels. That's us!

Or, to return to Bloy's metaphor, our Christian spirituality, as we try to live it in our ordinary, everyday lives, is one that makes heroes of us. Heroes, yes! Actually, it's never an either/or situation, as Buechner seems to suggest. It's more like both/and. Most of the time, we are both pigs *and* heroes, simultaneously.

As disciples of the risen Lord we need to give ourselves some credit. Instead of thinking of yourself as a slacker when it comes to faith and spirituality, step back and take a closer look. Do you not keep trying? Of course you do. You strive daily to keep your promises, big and small. If you are married, you try to love, honor, and cherish your spouse. If you have children, you feed and clothe them and put a roof over their knobby little heads. You hug your spouse and hug and teach your children, and you distribute kisses as appropriate. Now and then, you pray for them all, and for yourself, and for the poor old world.

In other words, you are a person who lives a Christian spirituality in practical ways, day in, day out. Look, that's why you have that halo hovering over your head there — tarnished, sure, but a halo all the same. That's why you have those angel wings beginning to sprout behind your shoulders — not yet big enough to fly with, true, but angel wings all the same. That's why you are a hero after God's own heart. So give yourself some credit.

A Spirituality for Lectors

Your Christian spirituality — which is virtually

indistinguishable from your lifestyle — expresses itself in many ways. You also nourish and neglect your spirituality in many ways. We all do. You nourish your spirituality by all the choices you make, from the kind of work you do and the attitude you do it with to the ways you use your leisure time. You nourish your spirituality by including prayer in your day in ways that are meaningful for you, by getting away for a retreat or day of prayerful solitude and reflection now and then. If you are married, your relationship with God cannot be separated from your relationship with your spouse, so your marriage is basic to your spirituality, too. There are also some important connections between your spirituality and the work you do.[2]

Of course, you also nourish and express your spirituality by participation in the eucharist, or Mass, and the other sacraments of the Church. Catholic spirituality is sacramental right down to its toes. Here we begin to see where being a lector fits into your spirituality and colors it in special ways. For a lector, of course, is one who carries out a particular ministry in the context of the Mass. Here is the special "twist" that being a lector gives to your spirituality: it highlights the place of the Scriptures in your life. Of course, every soul present for the eucharist participates in the Liturgy of the Word, and the word of God is addressed to all. But as a lector you become *the means by which the liturgy speaks God's word to the assembly.*

As a lector, therefore, intimacy with the scriptures takes on a special importance in your spirituality. If a lector's spirituality has a special characteristic, this would be it. This does not mean that as a lector you have some special obligation to become a walking, talking expert on the Bible. Hardly. But a lector does assume a special responsibility to have a good, adult understanding of what the Scriptures are and of their central message.

The spirituality of a lector is a spirituality nourished by the word of God. This means that as a lector you are called to give at least a few minutes each day to Scriptural prayer. This does not mean you need to adopt the lifestyle of a monk or cloistered nun. It does mean that you will become a more effective lector if you find a way to let the scriptures into your heart each day.

You may suppose that being a lector means that you need to become more interested in "things eternal" and less interested in "the things of this world." On the contrary. Cardinal John Henry Newman (1801-1890) once said: "I read my Bible to know what people ought to do and my newspaper to know what they are doing."[3]

In other words, greater familiarity with the Scriptures should make you more, not less, sensitive to the concerns of everyday life and of the world at large. Regular exposure to the word of God will not only help you to be a more effective lector, it will also help you to look upon the world

— and your little corner of it — with greater sensitivity to the need for, and presence of, goodness and peace, justice and truth, compassion and love. This is what the spirituality of a lector looks like.

1. Frederick Buechner, *The Alphabet of Grace* (New York: The Seabury Press, 1970), vii-viii.
2. See Mitch Finley, *101 Ways to Nourish Your Soul* (New York: The Crossroad Publishing Co., 1996).
3. Anthony Castle, *A Treasury of Quips, Quotes & Anecdotes for Preachers and Teachers* (Mystic, CT: Twenty-Third Publications, 1998), 43.

Chapter 1
THE SCRIPTURES AND YOU

AS A LECTOR, it is important to have a good basic understanding of the Scriptures — what they are, where they came from, and how to understand their meaning. As we noted earlier, you don't need to be a Scripture scholar to be a lector any more than you need to be a professional mechanic to drive a car. But just as a driver needs to have some basic driving skills and some general idea of how a car operates, so a lector needs a fundamental understanding of the Bible and how to read and interpret it accurately and with understanding.

A single chapter in a little book such as this one cannot hope to offer all you need to know about the Scriptures, of course.[1] All the same, we can at least look at some basic information to get you started, maybe spark your interest in further reading.

What is the Bible?

The Lectionary, from which a lector proclaims the Scriptural readings for a given day in the liturgical cycle, is simply a collection of readings taken from the Bible. We will talk more about the Lectionary in a subsequent chapter. For now, the important question is, what is the Bible?

Many people think of the Bible as one book,

but in fact the Bible is a collection of books, each one written in different historical and cultural circumstances, mostly in Hebrew or Greek, by one or more human authors under the inspiration of the Holy Spirit. The Bible is the word of God in human words, and it's important to take both parts of this description seriously. We should not try to pretend that the Bible is only "the word of God," as if God wrote or dictated the actual words in the original Hebrew or Greek manuscripts — much less the English translation we use.

When we say that the Scriptures are "inspired," this does not mean that every word in the original manuscripts was verbally spoken by God to the human author(s) who simply wrote down what God dictated. Some fundamentalist Jewish and Christian groups believe that this is what happened, more or less, but the Roman Catholic Church, the eastern Orthodox churches, and the mainline Protestant churches believe otherwise.[2]

As Catholics, we believe that God inspired the human authors of the scriptural documents, but He did not short-circuit their personalities and unique gifts, or enable them to transcend their time and place. Rather, God worked in and through the sacred authors. Does this mean that the Scriptures are free from all error, as some believe? If we believe that the Scriptures are inspired by God does this mean that they are all literally historical in the modern sense of the word? "It does not," wrote Father

Raymond E. Brown; "there can be inspired poetry, drama, legend, fiction, etc."[3]

In all cases, regardless of a document's literary form it can and does communicate truth *precisely by being* poetry, drama, legend, the unique literary form called "gospel," or whatever it may be. A modern example of this would be a newspaper comic strip. A "Peanuts" comic strip can communicate truth just as easily as a front page news story in that same newspaper, but each is a unique literary style.

One of the most common examples of how people misunderstand the Bible occurs in the creation accounts in the book of Genesis. People who read Genesis literally, as a historical and scientific document, must believe, contrary to all the available scientific evidence, that God created the universe in six, twenty-four-hour days. Catholic Scripture scholars explain, on the contrary, that Genesis was never meant to be a historical and scientific account in the modern sense. Rather, its literary style might be called "religious lore and legend."[4] Thus, we "still accept the creation of the world by God as the inspired truth conveyed by those chapters."[5] We do not, however, "have to accept the Genesis description as a scientific account of the origins of the world."[6] The point is that the author(s) of Genesis, who had not a clue about modern scientific theories, used "legend and lore" to communicate the divinely inspired truth that "God is sovereign of all and creator of the universe."[7]

This approach to interpreting the Scriptures respects the human intellect as a source of truth from which modern scientific insights come. At the same time, it respects the inspired truth communicated by Genesis. In other words, Catholicism does not ask us to shut down our intellect and ignore modern science in order to read the Bible.

Sometimes people are scandalized to learn that everything in the Bible is not literally, historically, scientifically true. But there is no need to be scandalized. The point is that the Bible is filled with many different literary styles by means of which divinely inspired truths are communicated to us.

Does this mean that Catholics deny the inerrancy of the Scriptures? No, but it does mean that our understanding of biblical inerrancy is far from simplistic. Father Raymond Brown: "The Bible teaches faithfully and without error that truth that God intended for the sake of our salvation, says Vatican Council II. . . I understand that to mean that in judging inerrancy we cannot simply ask what did the writer intend; we have to ask about the extent to which what the writer communicated is for the sake of our salvation."[8]

You need not look far to find information or statements in the Bible that have nothing to do with our salvation. With regard to our salvation, it doesn't matter *where* Jesus was born, only *that* Jesus was born. It doesn't matter exactly *how* Jesus' resurrection happened, only *that* Jesus' resurrection happened. It doesn't matter *how* God created the universe, only *that* God created the universe. And so forth. . .

The oldest books in the Bible are the Hebrew Scriptures or Old Testament. The documents written most recently constitute the Christian Scriptures or New Testament. The Old Testament predates Christianity, of course. Indeed, when the Gospels, the Letters of St. Paul, and other New Testament documents refer to "Scripture," the reference is to the Hebrew Scriptures.[9] These were the only sacred Scriptures, strictly speaking, that the Church had for the first two or three centuries of its existence. Indeed, the New Testament as we know it wasn't complete and accepted by the whole Church until 367 A.D. in the east, and 405 A.D. in the west.[10]

Sacred Scripture and Sacred Tradition

The New Testament is of particular interest to Christians, of course, because its documents originated with the unique, unrepeatable, foundational faith experiences of the Christian community. The key word here is "experience," because it was the faith experience of the early Church that gave birth to the New Testament. Another term for this ongoing faith experience is "tradition."

Actually, "tradition" has two theological meanings. The first meaning refers to the process of handing on the "memory, experience, expression and interpretation of the foundational self-revelation of God which was completed with Christ and the New Testament community."[11]

The second meaning of "tradition" refers to "the living heritage which is handed on."[12] In other words, the first meaning of "tradition" refers to tradition as *act,* while the second meaning refers to the *content* of tradition. Both meanings come into play to explain the origins of the New Testament and the circumstances under which we read and interpret the New Testament today.

Finally, we need to distinguish between Tradition and tradition(s):

> Tradition (uppercase) is the living and lived faith of the Church; traditions (lowercase) are customary ways of doing or expressing matters related to faith. If a tradition cannot be rejected or lost without distortion of the Gospel, it is part of Tradition itself. If a tradition is not essential (i.e., if it does not appear, for example, in the New Testament, or if it is not clearly taught as essential to Christian faith), then it is subject to change or even to elimination. It is not part of the Tradition of the Church.[13]

Sacred Scripture and Sacred Tradition cannot be separated, for they go hand-in-hand today just as they were united in the very beginning of Christianity. This is so because it was Sacred Tradition — the early Christian community's experience of the risen Christ in its midst and in the world — that conceived and gave birth to the New Testament. In other words, Sacred Tradition predated, was simultaneous with, and continued after the formation of the New Testament, right up to the present. Indeed, it is only in union with Sacred Tradition that we can read the scriptures in the spirit — and the Spirit — in which they were written.

"Sacred Tradition and Sacred Scripture. . .are bound closely together and communicate one with the other," declared the Second Vatican Council in 1965. "For both of them, flowing out from the same divine wellspring, come together in some fashion to form one thing and move towards the same goal."[14]

The Historical Character of the Scriptures

We need to take seriously the historical character of the Scriptures. We need to understand something about the historical and cultural circumstances in which the Scriptures were written in order to understand the meaning(s) intended by the human authors.

The Gospels, for example, are clearly the result of historical development. The Pontifical Biblical Commission, in its 1964 instruction, "Concerning the Historical Truth of the Gospels,"[15] explained this process. Basing its teaching on the research and consensus of twentieth century Scripture scholarship, the Commission declared that the Gospels went through a three-stage process of formation. The first stage was the time of the historical Jesus. The second stage was the time following the resurrection and ascension of Jesus when the oral traditions about Jesus developed. The third and final stage was the time during which the Gospels — blending the oral traditions, the contemporary faith experience of various Christian communities, and the theological insights of the evangelists — were written down. The other New Testament documents are the result of a similar process of historical development.

Why is it important for you, as a lector, to be aware of all this? It is important because having such knowledge has an impact on the attitude with which you approach the Scriptures and on the ways in which you prepare to proclaim the Scriptures during Mass.

Understanding that the word of God comes to us in historically and culturally conditioned human words affects your attitude. You should never approach the Scriptures with the assumption that the word of God is beyond your understanding, therefore the best you can do is read the words aloud and hope for the best. Rather, the divine meaning of the word of God is couched in its human meaning. Therefore, it is both possible and vitally important to learn something *about* the readings you proclaim before you do so.

We will go into more detail about practical ways to prepare to proclaim a particular reading or set of readings in Part II of this book. For now, however, we can provide some background information that will be helpful later.

As a lector, there are some resources you may want to have available. The first, and most useful, is a good study Bible, and you can't do better than *The Catholic Study Bible* (Oxford University Press, 1990). Any Catholic bookstore should have this edition of the Bible available, and any bookstore can order a copy for you.

Essentially, *The Catholic Study Bible* is the *New American Bible* (NAB), which is the translation used in the Lectionary. This volume includes, of course, the excellent footnotes that come with any edition of the NAB. But more important, it also includes excellent, informative Introductions to the books of the Bible, plus topical articles written for the average reader, all by Catholic Scripture scholars. *The Catholic Study Bible* offers you, the lector, a one-volume resource you can pick up and read quickly and easily as you prepare to proclaim a particular scriptural reading or set of readings.

If you want to have even more information at hand, consider owning a copy of *The New Jerome Biblical Commentary*, edited by Raymond E. Brown,

S.S., et al. (Prentice Hall, 1990). This hefty reference volume is far from inexpensive, but it is the best in-depth Bible commentary by Catholic scholars. As you prepare to proclaim the word of God, this book will give you all the background and interpretation of the readings anyone could want.

Finally, consider having your own copy of a good Bible dictionary. Here you can look up the definitions of particular words. Believe it or not, when as a lector you read aloud a word you don't understand that has a negative impact on how you read it. Still among the best is a book that has been around a long time, *Dictionary of the Bible*, by John L. McKenzie (Macmillan, 1965).

1. If you read only one book for a good basic understanding, I highly recommend *Responses to 101 Questions on the Bible*, by Raymond E. Brown, S.S. (Mahwah, NJ: Paulist Press, 1990). This and some other books you may find beneficial are listed in the Recommended Reading section at the end of this book.
2. For the fundamentalist viewpoint, see Harold Lindsell, *The Battle for the Bible* (Grand Rapids, MI: Zondervan Publishing House, 1976).
3. Brown, *Responses to 101 Questions on the Bible*, 31.
4. Ibid.
5. Ibid.
6. Ibid.
7. Ibid.
8. Ibid, 90. See the Vatican II *Dogmatic Constitution on Divine Revelation* 3:11.
9. See, for example, Romans 10:11. "The scripture says, 'No one who believes in him will be put to shame'." The reference is to Isaiah 28:16.

10. Metzger and Coogan, eds., *The Oxford Companion to the Bible,* 101-102.
11. Gerald O'Collins, S.J. and Edward G. Farrugia, S.J., *A Concise Dictionary of Theology* (Mahwah, NJ: Paulist Press, 1991), 246.
12. Ibid.
13. Richard P. McBrien, *Catholicism,* Revised Edition (San Francisco: HarperSanFrancisco, 1994), 63.
14. *Dogmatic Constitution on Divine Revelation,* n. 9.
15. "Instruction of the Pontifical Biblical Commission Concerning the Historical Truth of the Gospels, April 21, 1964," in James J. McGivern, ed., *Bible Interpretation* (Wilmington, DE: Consortium Books), 391-398.

Chapter 2

THE LITURGY OF THE WORD

As a lector, you have a special interest in that part of the Mass called the Liturgy of the Word. It will be helpful, then, if we examine this part of the Mass in some detail.

The Liturgy of the Word includes everything that happens in the Mass from the first reading through the Prayer of the Faithful. Actually, Liturgies of the Word, though sometimes quite brief, usually precede the celebration of all the sacraments and even sacramental blessings. This includes weddings and funerals — even when not celebrated in the context of a Mass — baptisms, and blessings of various kinds. The latter would include, for example, a blessing of animals on the feast of St. Francis of Assisi (October 4).

It may be helpful here to take a quick look at the parts of the Mass that lead up to the Liturgy of the Word so we can get a sense for the place of the Liturgy of the Word in the Mass as a whole. Later, we will examine the relation of the Liturgy of the Word to the Liturgy of the Eucharist.

The Liturgy of the Word belongs to a liturgical conversation, if you will, between God and the eucharistic assembly. There is even a kind of choreography involved. Not that the liturgy is a dance, of course, except by analogy. The point is that the focus of the eucharist shifts from one focal point to another, and back again in a kind of circular pattern, as the liturgy progresses. At the same time, the whole liturgy is centered on Christ, and each part of the liturgy draws our attention to his presence in our midst.

The Mass has four parts: the Introductory Rites, the Liturgy of the Word, the Liturgy of the Eucharist, and the Concluding Rites. The essentials may be summarized thus:

Sunday Masses, and Masses on the occasion of Solemnities, usually begin with an entrance song. On weekdays, however, the congregation instead sometimes recites an entrance antiphon — a short verse often, but not always, based on one of the Psalms.

Following the entrance song or antiphon, the priest convenes or gathers the congregation together by leading everyone in the sign of the cross.[1] He then extends a liturgical greeting, and there are three options to choose from: 1) "The grace of our Lord Jesus Christ and the love of God and the fellowship of the Holy Spirit be with you all." 2) "The grace and peace of God our Father and the Lord Jesus Christ be with you." 3) "The Lord be with you." Regardless of which option the priest uses, the congregation responds, "And also with you."[2]

Next comes the Penitential Rite. Here the focus of the liturgy shifts to the congregation's ongoing need for repentance and conversion. Using words supplied by the Sacramentary, the priest leads the eucharistic assembly through an admission of guilt, a petition for God's forgiveness, and a litany of praise for divine mercy. He then concludes with, "May almighty God have mercy on us, forgive us our sins, and bring us to everlasting life."[3]

During Sunday Masses, and Masses on Solemnities (except during Advent and Lent), the congregation then sings or recites the Gloria, or "Glory to God." Following a moment of silence, the priest then recites an opening prayer from the Sacramentary. Next comes the section of the liturgy we are most concerned with here.

A Liturgy of the Word is the public reading of scriptural texts, but it is far more than that. A Liturgy of the Word is one of the primary ways in which the risen Christ is present in the Church. In its *Constitution on the Sacred Liturgy* (1963), the Second Vatican Council declared that Christ "is present in his word since it is he himself who speaks when the holy Scriptures are read in the Church" (n. 7). This means that, as a lector, when you proclaim the Scriptures during the Liturgy of the Word, Christ speaks through you. By fulfilling the ministry of lector you *make Christ present* in a special and important way. This is a great privilege, indeed.

Think about this for a moment. You, the lector, are not merely someone who stands before the eucharistic assembly and reads aloud some sacred words from a printed page. When you proclaim the scriptural readings something happens — a great mystery — that would not happen if everyone in the congregation silently perused the readings for themselves — from a missalette, for example. It is understandable if some members of the congregation follow along in a missalette as you read aloud. But such reading is supplemental, for the sake of hearing more clearly, or as a way to bolster or magnify the experience of *hearing* the word of God proclaimed aloud.

The dynamic of *hearing* the Scriptures as they are read aloud, or *proclaimed,* in church in the context of the Mass, is the means by which Christ becomes present. Therefore, *how* you proclaim the Scriptures is vitally important to the quality of the experience for the entire congregation. But more about this later. . .

As Catholics, we understand that Christ is present in a special way through the proclamation of the word of God in the Scriptures. At the same time, "God's word is. . .also discerned in the words preached to and received by the assembly and in the Prayer of the Faithful, a proclamation and rehearsal of the Church's concern for others."[4]

Clearly, however, you have a unique role as you proclaim the word of God which is foundational to both the homily and the Prayer of the Faithful. Indeed, even if there is no homily — at a weekday Mass, for example — you make Christ present as you proclaim the word of God.

Back to our overview of the Liturgy of the Word: On Sundays and solemnities — such as Christmas and Easter — the Liturgy of the Word includes the following: a reading from the Old Testament; a response which consists of the singing or recitation of part of a psalm; a reading from one of the Letters of St. Paul, from a Letter by another New Testament author, from the Acts of the Apostles, or from the Book of Revelation; a Gospel acclamation; and finally a reading from one of the four Gospels. The presiding priest, concelebrating priest, or deacon proclaims the Gospel reading.

For weekday Masses, with few exceptions there are only two readings, the first from either the Hebrew Scriptures or a New Testament document other than a Gospel, the second from one of the Gospels, with a psalm response between the two. On weekdays, typically either there is a short homily or no homily at all. In most cases the Prayer of the Faithful is also included.

As noted above, the word of God is primarily a *spoken* word, not a word printed in ink on the pages of a book. Of course, we couldn't do without Bibles, and down through the centuries the printed word has made it possible to preserve the scriptural word of God. But the word of God is, first of all, a *spoken* word, a *dynamic* word, a "word" spoken to us *by God*. This is why the ministry of lector is so important to the liturgy.

As a lector, it is your ministry to proclaim the word of God. Or rather, it is your ministry to allow God to speak his word through you to the eucharistic assembly. When you proclaim the word of God it comes alive, and it is your role to let the word of God come alive in you so that it may come alive for the entire congregation.

As a lector, you become the means by which God's word touches the hearts of those gathered together for precisely this purpose. It is no easy thing to be an effective lector, however, for there are social obstacles to overcome and cultural challenges to meet. To begin with, we live in an era characterized by what early twentieth-century Catholic philosopher Max Picard called "verbal noise."[5] Picard's description of our situation is harsh:

> Instead of truly speaking to others today we are all waiting merely to unload on to others the words that have collected inside us. Speech has become a purely animal, excretive function.[6]

A moment's reflection on our own experience tells us that what Max Picard said is closer to the truth than we might like to admit. Many of the words we and others speak are little more than babble, "small talk," a spilling over of words in the service of our craving for attention. Often, this is the function of words today. At the same time, every day we are bombarded by even emptier words from even shallower sources.

The mass media advertising industry pummels us with words that have no connection to the human spirit. If anything, they drain the human spirit of life. From radio and television alone pours a torrent of words, words, words that tell not the truth but lies — attractive lies, it's true, but lies all the same. Ninety-nine percent of the words excreted by mass media advertising play on human needs and anxieties, and the thirst of the human heart, for one purpose: to sell everything from automobiles to beer, and from insurance policies to cat food and cosmetics.

This is the social and cultural context in which the Liturgy of the Word happens, in which you, the lector, make bold to stand up and speak a radically different kind of word, the word of God. In a world where people are pummeled with words of a far different kind day in, day out, however, the challenge for a lector is not insignificant. The truth is that the people you speak to often have numb ears because they are constantly pounded by Max Picard's "verbal noise." Frequently, the ears of the people who make up the eucharistic assembly are battered and bruised, at least in a spiritual sense. As a lector, it's important for you to keep this in mind and approach your ministry accordingly.

In a later chapter, we'll talk about practical steps you can take to help the congregation really hear the word of God. For now, we need to go deeper into the meaning and purpose of the Liturgy of the Word. First, recall the central place of "word" in the Scriptures. In the Bible, "the word of God" is a common expression for God's self-revelation; indeed, "the word" (of God) carries the divine Presence. Genesis 15:1 tells us, for example, that "the word of the Lord came to Abram in a vision." The "word of the Lord" has an almost physical presence.

In the New Testament, "word" is another term for the person of Christ himself. The clearest example of this is in the Prologue to John's Gospel:

> In the beginning was the Word, and the Word was with God, and the Word was God. He was in the beginning with God. All things came into being through him, and without him not one thing came into being. What has come into being in him was life, and the life was the light of all people (1:1-4).

Taking both of these ideas — the word of God as carrying the Presence of God, and the Word of God as Christ himself — we find ourselves smack in the middle of a great and holy mystery. If what you do as a lector is proclaim the word of God, then what you do as a lector is bring into the eucharistic assembly the Presence of God and, indeed, the person of Christ himself.

Perhaps we can compare what you do as a lector with what a priest does when he presides at the eucharist. In Matthew's Gospel, the risen Christ teaches his disciples that "where two or three are gathered in my name, I am there among them" (18:20). Therefore, we know that even before Mass begins, simply from the fact that we gather together, Christ is already truly present in our midst.

Perhaps it will be helpful to use a concept traditionally limited to the eucharistic bread and wine. We might say that the gathering of the faith community is the first way we experience "the real presence" of Christ. While the risen Christ's "real presence" in the consecrated bread and wine is unique and special, his presence in the assembled community is real, too.

The same is true when you proclaim the word of God during the Liturgy of the Word. Christ becomes truly present in another way, and you, the lector, are the means by which this happens. When you proclaim the word of God from the scriptures, Christ becomes present in the eucharistic assembly in a real and powerful way. To repeat words from Vatican II that we quoted before: "He is present in his word since it is he himself who speaks when the holy Scriptures are read in Mass."[7]

1. Currently, in parishes where no priest is in residence, often the lay parish administrator, pastoral associate, or deacon presides at a Communion Service. For an enlightening discussion of issues related to this phenomenon see James Dallen, *The Dilemma of Priestless Sundays* (Chicago: Liturgy Training Publi-

cations, 1994).

2. *The Sacramentary* (New York: Catholic Book Publishing Co., 1974), 359.

   In some cases, the priest may follow the liturgical greeting with an informal welcome not provided for in the Sacramentary. This may include a welcome for guests, strangers, and/or special groups present for this particular Mass. The priest may also, at this time, introduce the theme of the Mass about to be celebrated.

3. Ibid, 362.

4. Jeffrey T. Vanderwilt, "Liturgy of the Word," in Richard P. McBrien, general ed., *The HarperCollins Encyclopedia of Catholicism* (San Francisco: HarperSanFrancisco, 1995), 791.

5. Max Picard, *The World of Silence*, trans. by Stanley Godman (South Bend, IN: Regnery/Gateway, Inc., 1952), p. 172ff.

6. Ibid, 177.

7. *Constitution on the Sacred Liturgy*, n. 7.

Chapter 3

THE RELATIONSHIP BETWEEN THE LITURGY OF THE WORD AND THE LITURGY OF THE EUCHARIST

THERE IS AN ORGANIC CONNECTION between the Liturgy of the Word and the Liturgy of the Eucharist. If we give the Liturgy of the Word a second class status it is because we overlook its similarity to the Liturgy of the Eucharist and vice-versa. According to the Second Vatican Council, the Liturgy of the Word and the Liturgy of the Eucharist "are so closely connected with each other that they form but one single act of worship."[1]

In the Liturgy of the Word the risen Christ comes to us in words proclaimed from Sacred Scripture. In the Liturgy of the Eucharist the risen Christ comes to us in the consecrated bread and wine. In both cases we can speak of a "real presence." Christ is really present when the Scriptures are proclaimed. Christ is really present in the consecrated bread and wine of the eucharist. In the one, we receive Christ in words. In the other, we share Christ in the ritual meal called the eucharist. In both, the risen Christ is just as real, truly alive and active.

Ordinarily, of course, when we consume something it becomes part of us. When we eat ordinary food it nourishes us physically and becomes a part of our body. When we consume the risen Body and Blood of Christ in the eucharist, however, the process is reversed. Instead of your body transforming Christ into yourself, something else happens. In a mystical and real way, the eucharist nourishes your gradual transformation into the person of the risen Lord.

In a similar manner, when we listen to the words of Scripture proclaimed at Mass those words carry the presence of the risen Christ, and that presence changes us from the inside out. Instead of us "consuming" the presence of Christ, when the word of God is proclaimed at Mass the effect is to nourish and transform us. This is true both for the faith community that receives God's word and for the individuals who make up that community.

Both the Liturgy of the Word and the Liturgy of the Eucharist are personal encounters with the risen Lord. In the one we meet Christ in the Scriptural word of God. In the other, we meet Christ as he gives himself to us in the bread and wine of the eucharist. It is one and the same Christ that we receive in both. As we suggested earlier, if Catholics tend to have less of an appreciation for receiving Christ in the proclamation of Scripture, it may be because for so many generations — following the sixteenth-century Protestant Reformation which emphasized the Bible and de-emphasized the eucharist — Catholicism gave more attention to the eucharist than to the Scriptures.

This is not to say that Catholicism lost touch entirely with the need for good preaching. By no means. The Counter-Reformation included, for example, a great many itinerant preachers such as the Dominicans and Franciscans. But Catholicism did give less attention to the public proclamation of the Scriptures as a vital part of the Mass. Consequently, Catholics lost a certain sensitivity to the presence of Christ in the liturgical proclamation of the word of God that we are regaining today.

One way to restore this sensitivity to the real presence of Christ in the proclamation of the Scriptures is to recall that the same Christ is present in both word and sacrament. When it comes to Scripture, however, we may wonder how Christ can be present in a word — or, to be more precise, in *human words*. Certainly, the words of Scripture are the word of God, but theologians tell us that we can't just say "Scripture is the word of God" and leave it at that. As theologian Bernard Cooke wrote:

> Since it is obvious that words can operate as words only when there is some process of actual communication between persons, the text of the Bible by itself cannot be word of God; it can function as word only when it is being used to convey some understanding to a believing individual or community.[2]

To put this another way, a "word" becomes a "word" only when it carries *meaning.* For example, if you are not familiar with certain technical terms, and someone asks you to obtain a "counter-threaded terminus frazzledasher," this "word" isn't really a word for you because it means nothing. As soon as that same person explains the meaning of this term, however, then what he or she says or writes becomes a real "word" for you, because now it has *meaning.*

In a similar way, the words of Scripture become true "words" for you only when they *mean* something to you. If you had never heard of God, or if you had never heard of Jesus, and someone read to you from the Gospel of Luke the story of the Good Samaritan, it would not be "word of God" for you until "God" and "Jesus" first had some meaning for you. Indeed, it would become "word of God" only when you had a faith relationship with God and with Christ. Then the story would make sense; then it would be not just an inspirational story but "the word of God," which is something different and far more powerful.

To say that the Scriptures "are the word of God" can be misleading, therefore, because the Scriptures are "word of God" only when we read them in the context of human faith experience. "Somehow human experience and Bible together form 'word of God'."[3] If the Scriptures are God's self-revelation to us, then we must say that divine revelation happens not in the words of Scripture, per se, but in the *encounter* between us and the word of God in Scripture. This is why the ministry of lector is so important, for it is the lector's role in the liturgy to be the *means* by which this encounter happens between the eucharistic assembly and the Scriptures.

It may be helpful to borrow language from the Prologue to the Gospel of John, which refers to Christ as "the Word" (1:1). It is Christ as "the Word" that we receive when a lector proclaims the Scriptural readings at Mass. But it is the same Christ, who is "the Word," that we receive in Holy Communion. Again, the risen Christ is the same in both instances, and we receive him in different forms — as word and as consecrated bread and wine. But it is one and the same Christ that we receive in both the proclamation of Scripture and in Holy Communion.

The *Catechism of the Catholic Church* points out that the movement from word to eucharist is the same as that experienced by the disciples with the risen Jesus. "Walking with them he explained the Scriptures to them; sitting with them at table 'he took bread, blessed and broke it, and gave it to them'."[4]

The Spirit that unites the Liturgy of the Word and the Liturgy of the Eucharist is the same in both parts of the Mass. Therefore, we not only miss the boat, but we slip and fall off the pier if we think of the Liturgy of the Word as a mere preface to or preparation for the Liturgy of the Eucharist. In fact, both are high points of the Mass. If the Liturgy of the Word has a progression of its own, however, we would need to say that the Scriptural readings themselves are the high point, not the homily. One authority on liturgy compares the Liturgy of the Word to a mountain, saying that, "The final element in the downward slope of the mountain occurs in the homily. . ."[5]

The role of the lector is, therefore, far from incidental to the meaning and purpose of the Mass as a whole. Sometimes we hear people speak of the priest as the one who "says Mass" or "celebrates the eucharist." While there can be no Mass without the priest, of course, and it is theologically possible for a priest to "say Mass" in private, the old custom of private Masses is practically a thing of the past. This is because there is a real way in which the congregation as a whole "says Mass" or "celebrates the eucharist." The priest presides at the eucharist, he doesn't "say Mass" with the congregation serving as mere spectators. The entire congregation celebrates the eucharist; it isn't an activity for spectators.

This is why it is so important for the entire congregation to take an active part in the Mass. This is one reason that the ministries of lector and eucharistic minister are important not only for the function they serve but also because they symbolize the active involvement of the entire assembly, not just the priest, in the celebration of the eucharist. When lay persons serve as lectors and eucharistic ministers they serve on behalf of all of us, reminding us by their presence and actions that all of us celebrate the eucharist *together* as a community.

Returning to the specific role of lector, however, it may be helpful to again compare the lector's role in the Liturgy of the Word with the priest's role in the Liturgy of the Eucharist. As we saw above, we can't strictly speak of the Scriptures, in the sense of printed-words-on-pages, as "the word of God." Rather, the word of God occurs in the encounter between the words of Scripture and the faith of those who hear, or read, those words. Consequently, there is a sense in which we can say that what you do as lector is to facilitate this encounter. You facilitate the real presence of the word of God for the assembly.

We might say that as a lector what you do is similar to what the priest does when he consecrates the eucharistic bread and wine. He facilitates the transformation of bread and wine into the body and blood, or whole person, of the risen Christ.[6] You, as lector, facilitate the transformation of Scriptural words-on-page into the actual word of God present in the encounter between spoken Scriptural words and the faith of the eucharistic assembly. You can see, then, why the ministry of lector is anything but incidental to the celebration of the Mass as a whole.

In a wonderful essay, the late Catholic fiction writer and essayist André Dubus used a surprising and delightful phrase. Dubus re-tells the post-Resurrection story of the two disciples on the road to Emmaus, in the Gospel of Luke (24:13ff). When he gets to the part where the risen Lord explains the Scriptures to the disciples, Dubus says that Jesus "teaches them the Scriptures they already know. . ."

This is a beautiful description of the Liturgy of the Word and its inherent purpose. In the Liturgy of the Word the risen Christ, present in the eucharistic assembly, teaches us the Scriptures *we already know.* It is the role of the lector to proclaim the Scriptures in such a way that the risen Lord may teach us the Scriptures we already know.[7]

Very often, most of the people in the congregation are familiar with the readings used for a particular Mass. In some instances the lector might think, with good reason, that all he or she needs to do is read the first sentence or two, and just about anyone in the congregation could recite the rest of the reading from memory. While this may be true, we need to keep in mind that the Scriptures are a never-ending source of meaning and insight. A line from one of the letters of St. Paul heard countless times can suddenly come alive with heretofore undiscovered meaning. A familiar verse from one of the Psalms can touch the heart unexpectedly. In other words, the Scriptures are simultaneously ancient and ever new, and it is the lector's role to proclaim the readings as if they had never been proclaimed before.

Just as we receive the same sacrament in Holy Communion time after time, over and over, so the risen Christ speaks to us through the Liturgy of the Word time after time, over and over again. As we saw at the beginning of this chapter, these two parts of the liturgy, these two experiences, are intimately connected. For historical reasons, however, many Catholics have less of an appreciation for the Liturgy of the Word than they do for the Liturgy of the Eucharist. The challenge for you as a lector, therefore, is to proclaim the readings from Scripture in a eucharistic manner.

What does it mean to proclaim the readings in a eucharistic manner? Recall that "eucharist" comes from a Greek word meaning "to give thanks." So the first meaning of this idea is to proclaim the readings with a thankful heart. If you are thankful for the word of God in your own life, it will show in how you proclaim the readings. You don't just "read aloud" some words from a printed page. You speak the words from a heart thankful for your faith, thankful for God's love, thankful for the gift of life. This is what it means, most basically, to proclaim the readings in a eucharistic manner.

Just as important, however, is your awareness that when you proclaim the readings Christ speaks through you. When you proclaim the Scriptures Christ becomes present in a fresh, new way in the eucharistic assembly. To proclaim the readings in a eucharistic manner means doing so out of a deep awareness that this is what you are doing.

The purpose of this book so far has been to reflect on the meaning and purpose of being a lector. It is critical to understand what you are about as a lector. But equally important are the practical skills you need as a lector. We now turn to the more practical side of the lector's ministry.

1. *The Constitution on the Sacred Liturgy* (1963), n. 56.
2. Bernard Cooke, *Ministry to Word and Sacraments: History and Theology* (Philadelphia: Fortress Press, 1976), 320.
3. Ibid.
4. *Catechism of the Catholic Church* (Washington, D.C.: United States Catholic Conference / Libreria Editrice Vaticana, 1994), n. 1347. See Luke 24:13-35.
5. Joseph M. Champlin, *The Mystery and Meaning of the Mass* (New York: The Crossroad Publishing Co., 1999), 69.
6. See Mitch Finley, *The Joy of Being a Eucharistic Minister* (Mineola, NY: Resurrection Press, 1998).
7. André Dubus, "Communion," in *Meditations From a Movable Chair* (New York: Alfred A. Knopf, 1998), 158.

PART II

PROCLAIMING THE WORD OF GOD EFFECTIVELY

MORE THAN LIKELY, at some time in your young life you learned to ride a bicycle. Of course, once you learn this skill it's something you don't lose or forget. No matter how long since you last climbed onto a bike, you can balance, pedal, and ride anytime you want to. That is because once you gain certain skills they stay with you. The same is true of being a lector. Sometimes people think they can just stand up and start reading aloud, and that's all there is to it. On the contrary, there are some basic skills you need to learn in order to carry out the ministry of lector effectively.

Have you ever learned to play a musical instrument? In order to play anything from piano to violin, from tuba to timpani, from banjo to bassoon, you can only learn by beginning at the beginning, one step at a time. If you want to play the clarinet, first you need to learn where to place your fingers for the various notes, and you learn only a few notes at a time. As a beginner, you play simple little three- or four-note songs. You begin to learn breath control and how to blow into the delicate reed in the clarinet's mouthpiece. After many hours of practice,

practice, practice you begin to play better and better.

The same principle holds true about being a lector. You need some basic skills, and you can only begin at the beginning. It won't take you as long to be an effective lector as it takes to learn to play the banjo, but the principles are the same: learn the basics, and practice and practice. Be open-minded about constructive criticism. Be willing to put some time into it. Don't expect to be the best lector you can be your first time up any more than you would expect to be a virtuoso oboe player the first time you pick up the instrument or an expert driver the first time you climb behind the wheel of an automobile.

One of the best ways to learn about being a good lector is to watch other lectors. Learn from those who do it well, and learn from those still learning to do it well. Watch, listen, and learn. Take advantage of opportunities to improve your lectoring skills. Practice at home with a tape recorder, then listen to how you sound. What can you do to improve?

There are five skills you need to work on in order to become an effective lector. They are:

1. Understand what you are going to read before the liturgy begins.
2. Speak clearly.
3. Take the sound system into account.

4. Read at a steady pace, not too fast, not too slow.

5. Read with expression.

Let's look at each skill in some detail:

1. Understand what you are going to read before the liturgy begins. If you are called on to lector at the last minute because the scheduled lector didn't show up, there is no chance to prepare. This happens sometimes, and there is nothing you can do about it. Otherwise, however, always prepare ahead of time. Locate the Scriptural passages you will be reading in your own Bible at home, being sure that you read the *New American Bible,* the same translation used in the Lectionary. If you have a calendar that includes liturgical information, it's easy to learn what the readings for a given Sunday or weekday Mass will be.[1]

Make the time to prepare well. Read slowly through the reading(s) you will be doing. If you come across a word or phrase you honestly do not understand, stop, get out your Bible dictionary or commentary, and do a little research. You may not think it makes any difference, but it affects the quality of your reading negatively if you don't understand what you are reading. We will go into this in more detail in Chapter 5.

2. Speak clearly. In our everyday speaking we tend to have "lazy mouth." We don't articulate our words clearly, we slur, we use poor grammar and slang, and all this may be fine for everyday, around-the-house purposes. But when you stand in front of the eucharistic assembly to proclaim the word of God, that's a whole different situation. Now it is important to read each word clearly and articulate distinctly. The point is not to read in a way that sounds artificial. Reading in a stilted, artificially distinct manner is just as distracting as if you were to rush through the reading and slur your words. The ideal is to read in a clear but natural manner, articulating the words clearly.

3. *Take the sound system into account.* In any parish church of any size today, there will be a microphone at the lectern — which, to be "liturgically correct," is called an "ambo." Every sound system is unique, so it is important to learn to use properly the one you will be using. Some mikes are extremely sensitive, which means you don't want it too close to your lips as you speak. Other mikes won't pick up your voice unless you practically have the thing in your mouth. All you can do is experiment and make sure you take into account the peculiarities of the sound system you will be using. Ideally, there will be opportunities for you to practice with your parish church's sound system outside of actual liturgical situations.

In situations where there is no sound amplification system, take the acoustics of the church, chapel, or room into account. Even in a small space, however, it is important to speak up, speak clearly, and articulate clearly. Keep your head up so your words are not muffled by being bounced off the pages of the Lectionary.

4. *Read at a steady pace, not too fast, not too slow.* What's too fast? What's too slow? New lectors sometimes read too fast, due perhaps to being a bit nervous. More experienced lectors sometimes read too fast because they slip into a "slap-dash" approach to lectoring: get up there, get through it, and get back to the pew. It's better to read a little too slowly than to read too fast. The ideal is a natural, unrushed reading pace. If you read too slow, that will distract people as much as reading too fast, but it's the rare lector for whom this is a problem. For most of us, it would improve the quality of our lectoring if we could slow down a little. Rely on the judgment of those who listen to you. If they think you read too fast, slow down. If they think you read too slow, pick up the pace a bit.

5. *Read with expression.* We will talk about this in more detail later in the book, but for now just realize that it's important for the lector to not read in a boring monotone. If you are, or have ever been, a parent or teacher to young children, you can apply this experience to your lectoring technique. When you read aloud to a young child you try to put some life into what you read.

From little wordless picture books designed for pre-verbal infants and children, to Margaret Wise Brown's classic *Good Night Moon;* from the Berenstain Bear books to Tolkien's *The Hobbit,* when you read aloud to kids you need to put some lively expression in your voice. You use a different tone for each character, perhaps. You vary your style depending on the kind of book you read. Your voice sounds different when you read *Peter Rabbit* than it does when you read *Little House on the Prairie.*

Apply these insights to your ministry as a lector. Let the literary style of the reading have an impact on how you read it. A narrative, such as the story of David and Bathsheba (2 Samuel 11:1-27), requires a different voice than a hymn, such as St. Paul's ode to Christ:

> Let the same mind be in you that was in Christ Jesus, who, though he was in the form of God, did not regard equality with God as something to be exploited, but emptied himself, taking the form of a slave, being born in human likeness. And being found in human form, he humbled himself and became obedient to the point of death — even death on a cross. Therefore God also highly exalted him and gave him the name that is above every name, so that at the name of Jesus every knee should bend, in heaven and on earth and under the earth,

and every tongue should confess that Jesus Christ is Lord, to the glory of God the Father (Philippians 2:5-10).

Let your voice reflect your understanding of what you read. Whatever you do, avoid reading with a dull monotone voice. Read as if what you are reading has meaning for you, personally. At the same time, there are always two extremes. Do not try to dramatize the reading or exaggerate so your reading comes across as weird or quirky.

The best advice anyone can give you is to read from your heart, not from your head. Proclaim the Scriptures from your deepest center where God dwells in silence and unconditional love. When you do that, those upon whose ears the sacred words fall will perceive what they are supposed to perceive: God speaking to them in the silence of their own hearts with a message of unconditional love.

1. The *Word and Worship Desk Calendar* or *Pocket Calendar* (Paulist Press, 1-800-218-1903) is an excellent, affordable calendar of this type.

Chapter 4
GETTING TO KNOW
THE LECTIONARY

AS A LECTOR, your main resource is a collection of readings, or "lessons," selected from the Bible and arranged according to the liturgical calendar for public reading at Mass. This book is called the Roman Lectionary.

We can trace the origins of the Lectionary we use today to our Jewish roots. Early Christian communities inherited from the synagogue the concept of assigning specific scriptural readings to specific feasts and Sabbaths. Prior to the Council of Nicaea, in 325, an actual Lectionary existed only for feast days while Sunday readings simply followed a plan for a continuous reading from particular books of the Bible, one book after the other. One selection would be read each Sunday until the particular book had been read clear through. Early on, several selections from both the Old and New Testaments were read, interspersed with selections from the Psalms. By the sixth century, in the Roman Church the readings were limited to two.[1]

The revised Roman Lectionary of 1969 — updated and revised again in 1997 — provides for three readings on Sundays and feast days. There are three year-long Sunday cycles of readings called

Year A, Year B, and Year C. These assign the Gospels of Matthew, Mark, and Luke in a more-or-less continuous fashion over the three-year cycle. John's Gospel is, for the most part, reserved for feasts and the liturgical seasons of Advent, Christmas, Lent, and Easter. Readings taken from John also fill in gaps that remain after the Gospel of Mark — the shortest of the Gospels — comes to an end. The Bible translation approved for use in the Lectionary in the United States today is the *New American Bible* with Revised New Testament, published in 1986. In other English-speaking countries the Church uses locally approved translations.

In the Lectionary, the first reading is usually from the Old Testament and is matched as closely as possible, thematically, with that day's Gospel reading. A responsorial psalm follows the first reading. The second reading, taken from one of the Letters of Saint Paul or from another non-gospel New Testament document, has no thematic connection to the other two readings.

Since the early to mid-1980s, the Lectionary has been the center of controversy, at least in certain circles. This controversy resulted from a concern for inclusive language in the Lectionary. Some people were offended by Scriptural references to God that used masculine pronouns ("he," "him") and by references to all people that relied on "man," "men," or "brothers," thus seeming to exclude females. In some instances, parish leaders or lectors would change the wording of the readings themselves, and this would irritate or anger some members of the congregation who objected that no one had a right to change the wording of the Bible.

Translators who worked on the most recent revision of the Lectionary had three objectives in mind: "maximum fidelity to the biblical text, greater ease in proclamation, and accurate translation of gender-inclusive scriptural terms."[2] As it turned out, the third of these goals proved to be the most difficult to achieve.

The experts who worked on the Lectionary revised the scriptural translation in more than three hundred instances in order to bring a greater sense of inclusivity.[3] In all instances, the original Greek or Hebrew texts allowed for these revisions while remaining faithful to the original texts. The ultimate goal of the new Lectionary was the greatest possible fidelity to the scriptural texts. When the biblical text is not gender specific, the Lectionary is not gender specific. When the biblical text is gender specific, the Lectionary is gender specific. Those responsible for the Lectionary did not believe they had the authority to actually change the biblical text.

These revisions went too far for some, not far enough for others. Still, it seems only right that any revisions made to adapt the Scriptures to contemporary cultural conditions must respect the historical character of the Scriptures. We can't pretend that the Scriptures were written yesterday. It is the task of the homilist to apply the readings to the present era. No lector should take it upon himself or herself to change the wording of a given reading because he or she finds it personally objectionable, for whatever reason. As a lector, you are obliged to proclaim the biblical reading exactly as it appears in the Lectionary.

If a lector decides to change the wording of a biblical passage it's as if he or she is saying, "I know what's best for everyone, and what's best for everyone is my opinion about this wording and my point of view about it." To impose my personal ideology on an entire congregation in this manner would be arrogant and self-serving at the very least.

The words I want to change may or may not need to be changed, but in the context of the liturgy I have no business imposing my ideological position on the entire congregation. Better to admit that the Scripture scholars, language experts, and liturgical experts who produced the Lectionary may have some knowledge, insights and, yes, authority that I do not. A little humility never hurt anyone. If certain parts of the readings are unclear or appear to be out of synch with contemporary sensitivities, the homily is the proper place for this to be dealt with.

As we already noted above, each Mass has three readings: the first from the Hebrew Scriptures or Old Testament, the second from one of the Epistles, the Acts of the Apostles, or the Book of

Revelation, and the third from one of the four Gospels. These readings are arranged according to a three-year cycle, so they are repeated every fourth year.

For weekday Masses, the Gospels are strung together to form a single year-long series of readings. Ordinary Time includes thirty-four weeks, and during this time there are two cycles of first readings, Series I for odd years, Series II for even years. During Advent, Christmas, Lent, and Easter there are readings unique to those seasons.

When saints' feast days occur, for some saints there are special readings. For other saints there are various readings from which to choose. The Lectionary also includes a wide selection of readings for use on special occasions such as marriages and funerals, Masses for special occasions such as a Mass of the Sacred Heart or a Mass of the Blessed Virgin Mary.

If you compare the readings in the Lectionary with the same passages in a copy of the Bible, you will see that in the Lectionary the readings are laid out in sense line order with indentations. This was done by experts on proclaiming the Scriptures to help make the lector's task easier. The sense lines are arranged to facilitate an accurate presentation of the inherent meaning of the reading. Does this mean that you should pause at the end of each sense line? Not necessarily. A sentence is still a sentence. If no punctuation, such as a comma, semicolon, or hyphen, appears at the end of a sense line, virtually no pause should occur as you read aloud for the congregation.

Often the readings in the Lectionary are slightly edited versions of the Scriptural texts. For example, the first reading for the Nineteenth Sunday in Ordinary Time (Year B) is 1 Kings 19:9a, 11-13a. If you locate these verses in the *New American Bible*, here is what you will find:

> [9] There he came to a cave, where he took shelter. But the word of the Lord came to him, "Why are you here, Elijah?" [10] He answered: "I have been most zealous for the Lord, the God of hosts, but the Israelites have forsaken your covenant, torn down your altars, and put your prophets to the sword. I alone am left, and they seek to take my life." [11] Then the Lord said, "Go outside and stand on the mountain before the Lord; the Lord will be passing by." A strong and heavy wind was rending the mountains and crushing rocks before the Lord — but the Lord was not in the wind. After the wind there was an earthquake — but the Lord was not in the earthquake. [12] After the earthquake there was fire — but the Lord was not in the fire. After the fire there was a tiny whispering sound. [13] When he heard this, Elijah hid his face in his cloak and went and

stood at the entrance of the cave.

Compare this to the same verses as they appear in the Lectionary:

> At the mountain of God, Horeb, Elijah came to a cave where he took shelter. Then the Lord said to him, "Go outside and stand on the mountain before the Lord; the Lord will be passing by." A strong and heavy wind was rending the mountains and crushing rocks before the Lord — but the Lord was not in the wind. After the wind there was an earthquake — but the Lord was not in the earthquake. After the earthquake there was fire — but the Lord was not in the fire. After the fire there was a tiny whispering sound. When he heard this, Elijah hid his face in his cloak and went and stood at the entrance of the cave.

Notice that at the beginning of the reading the editors of the Lectionary modified the actual biblical text for the sake of clarity. They inserted Elijah's name in verse 9a so we know right away who the story is about. They added information about Eliljah's location on Mount Horeb so we know where the event happened. The editors also left out both the second part of verse 9 and all of verse 10 because the information in these lines makes no sense, out of context, to the narrative we are about to hear. The editors also end the reading in the middle of verse 13 because the second half of that verse is a lead-in to the following verses and would be confusing if it were included in the reading.

You can see, therefore, that the Lectionary is not merely a collection of readings from the Bible, lifted "as is" and dropped into the Lectionary. Rather, the Lectionary is a unique volume that, whenever necessary, adapts the biblical readings to the liturgical context in which they will be proclaimed. Without changing the Scriptural meanings, the editors of the Lectionary add words and delete other words — sometimes they remove whole verses — all for the sake of clarity and understanding.

What? You may ask. They change the Bible? Can they do that? Not to get excited. The Lectionary is not the Bible; it's a selection of slightly edited readings *from* the Bible. The editors do not re-write the Bible, they simply provide the faith community with understandable excerpts from the Bible for use in liturgical celebrations. In no case will you find that editorial tinkering has anything but a positive and beneficial effect given the purpose the Lectionary is designed to serve. If the editors of the Lectionary did not make minor changes to the texts, quite often the readings would be unclear, puzzling, or misleading. As a lector, it's good for you to know that this happens so you are that much better informed.

What, then, *is* the Lectionary? The Lectionary is a resource, a means, not an end in itself. The Lectionary is a tool, if you will, used by the Church — the body of Christ, the people of God — to facilitate its liturgical encounter or interaction with the word of God. As we saw earlier, the word of God happens in the meeting of Scriptures and faith community. So the Lectionary is a resource that helps that meeting to happen.

1. See John A. Melloh, "Lectionary," in Richard P. McBrien, general editor, *The HarperCollins Encyclopedia of Catholicism* (San Francisco: HarperSanFrancisco, 1995), 762.
2. Joseph M. Champlin, *The Mystery and Meaning of the Mass* (New York: The Crossroad Publishing Co., 1999), 59.
3. Ibid.

Chapter 5

PREPARING TO PROCLAIM
THE WORD

HERE IS WHAT MAY SEEM LIKE a terribly abstract idea, but actually it's quite simple: The ministry of lector is a ministry of the word of God. But, as we have seen, the word of God is not merely sentences printed on biblical or Lectionary pages. Rather, the word of God comes to us in the encounter between faith — intimacy with the risen Christ — and human words — historically, culturally conditioned human words. That is, we experience God's "word" in a personal encounter and dialogue with the historically and culturally conditioned Scriptures.

Therefore, if we are to hear the actual word of God it is essential for us to take seriously the historical and culturally conditioned character of the Scriptural words. Otherwise, we may all too easily misunderstand or misinterpret Scriptural words and so miss the word of God entirely or understand it only in part. As perhaps the greatest Catholic Bible scholar of our time, the late Father Raymond E. Brown explained, "*word* of God (since God does not really speak in words) means a divine communication in human words spoken and written by people who had limited knowledge and restricted worldview and were facing specific problems."[1]

We need, always, to seek a good human understanding and prayerful experience of a given Scriptural reading in order for the divine communication to happen. Especially for a lector, it is important to prepare well, in practical terms, prior to proclaiming God's word in the context of the eucharistic liturgy.

A good preparation has three parts: 1) Reading; 2) Learning; 3) Prayer. You might want to divide the process into three separate sessions, perhaps three evenings during the week prior to the Sunday or Saturday evening you are scheduled to serve as lector. Keep in mind, also, that we are not talking about a huge time investment. Each part of the preparation process need not take more than ten or fifteen minutes. Let's look at each part in some detail.

Reading

The first step in preparing to exercise your ministry as a lector is to identify the reading(s) for which you are responsible. You can find this information on any calendar that includes liturgical information, and you can obtain such a calendar from any Catholic book store.[2] Often, calendars distributed free by parishes also include this information, as do daily devotional publications such as *Living Faith* and *My Daily Visitor*.[3]

The advantage of such a resource is that it indicates the readings for both Sundays and weekdays.

You may also find this information in a copy of the missalette used by your parish, but most parishes do not appreciate it when people take copies of the missalette home. Parish staff responsible for giving lectors the support they need should make sure that lectors have a way to know, well in advance, which readings they are to proclaim so they can prepare well.

An excellent source of information about the readings for Sundays only is *The Catholic Study Bible*.[4] This Bible includes an appendix, "The New 3-Year Cycle of Readings for Sunday Mass," which tells you the Sunday readings through the year 2014. Since *The Catholic Study Bible* is an outstanding resource for lectors for more reasons than this one, I highly recommend that lectors obtain a copy of this edition of the Bible.

Sometimes, you will find words with uncertain pronunciations. Many a lector gets tongue-tied over "Nebuchadnezzar." Now and then during a Good Friday service a lector pronounces the name of the high priest Annas as one would pronounce the name of a certain part of the human anatomy, and the entire congregation ends up trying to stifle hysterical laughter. Probably the easiest way to deal with difficult-to-pronounce words is to ask someone else who ought to know. There are Old Testament names and terms, however, that you hear pronounced various ways, so your best move is to use the pronunciation that seems most likely to you.

Once you identify the reading(s) for which you are responsible, the next step is to slowly and silently read to yourself what you will later proclaim aloud during Mass. After you read through the portion of Scripture for which you are responsible. . . read it again. As you read, be alert to the meaning of what you read. Does it make sense to you? Are there any words or terms that you honestly do not understand? Of the material you think you understand, is there anything you find perplexing or with which you are uncomfortable? Anything you especially like? Let's take an example. Say the first reading includes the following lines from the Letter of St. Paul to the Romans:

> For those who live according to the flesh are concerned with the things of the flesh, but those who live according to the spirit with the things of the spirit. The concern of the flesh is death, but the concern of the spirit is life and peace. For the concern of the flesh is hostility toward God; it does not submit to the law of God, nor can it; and those who are in the flesh cannot please God. But you are not in the flesh; on the contrary, you are in the spirit, if only the Spirit of God dwells in you. Whoever does not have the Spirit of Christ does not belong to him. But if Christ is in you, although the body is dead because of sin, the spirit is

alive because of righteousness. If the Spirit of the one who raised Jesus from the dead dwells in you, the one who raised Christ from the dead will give life to your mortal bodies also, through his Spirit that dwells in you (8:5-11).

As you read through these words you may be perplexed by Paul's remarks about "flesh" and "spirit" and "mortal bodies." Perhaps you squirm at what he says about "flesh" and "spirit" being at odds with each other. Perhaps you must admit that you are not sure what Paul is trying to say here. This should lead naturally into the next phase.

Learning

If you were to read the passage above from *The Catholic Study Bible* you would find much clarity from the footnote to verses 1-13. This footnote explains that "the flesh" is not a reference to the human body or, more specifically, to the human appetites for food, sex, and so forth. "Flesh" (Greek, *sarx*) is the term St. Paul uses to talk about "the old self," that is, "self-interested hostility toward God." The footnote goes on to explain that, "Christians still retain the flesh ["the old self"], but it is alien to their new being, which is life in the spirit, namely the new self, governed by the holy Spirit."[5]

This should help you to better understand what Paul says in Romans 8 about "flesh" and "spirit." When he uses the word "flesh," he means any behavior that expresses "self-interested hostility toward God." Or, for that matter, toward other people, too. This makes it possible for you to proclaim this reading with more understanding, in a more intelligent manner. Later, in the homily, the priest or deacon should pass along this information to the congregation, but that is not your concern as a lector. Still further insights may be gained if you consult a Bible dictionary, a Bible commentary, the Reading Guides in *The Catholic Study Bible*, and/or other translations of the Bible.[6] The more information you can gather about the reading(s) you will proclaim, the better your understanding will be.

The ideal is to learn as much as you can about the reading(s) you will proclaim. Of course, there are limits. For one thing, you have a limited amount of time for this learning phase. At the very least, however, you should consult your copy of *The Catholic Study Bible* to see what information you can gather from footnotes, Introductions, and Reading Guides.

Only when it is absolutely unavoidable should you approach the lectern or ambo to proclaim the word of God without giving some time to *learning about* the reading(s) you proclaim. It is understandable that now and then you may be called upon at the last minute to serve as lector. This may happen, for example, when the lector scheduled to serve at a particular Mass falls ill, or simply does not show up. In a situation such as this, the very least you can do is take a minute to go over the reading(s) you will be responsible for, to familiarize yourself with the words. This way, at least you are more likely to proclaim the reading smoothly and with some familiarity.

If these three steps might be called "proximate preparation," there is another form of preparation we might call "remote preparation." One of the best ways to be prepared for situations where you have no chance to learn *about* the reading(s) is to cultivate an ongoing interest in learning about the Scriptures in general. There are some excellent books available at your local religious bookstore that can help you become better informed about the Scriptures, and a good place to begin is with the Recommended Reading section at the end of this book. Also, you can attend Scripture classes offered by parishes. Such an ongoing interest in learning about the Scriptures is "remote preparation" or "continuing education," and you can do it anytime.

Now for the third and final part of the preparation process which, in a very real sense, is the most important part even though the first two parts are essential.

Prayer

After you read slowly through the reading(s) you are responsible for a couple of times; and after you do a little research to clarify meanings of words and ideas, then it is time to spend a few minutes just being with the scriptural readings in a prayerful way.

You need to discover a way that is best for you, personally, to do this. Not everyone will find the same approach helpful. One way to pray with the scriptures is called *Lectio Divina*, which simply means "holy reading." It's possible to practice this ancient method of prayer in a highly structured manner, but it's also possible to simplify it, and this simple approach may be best for our purposes.

Here is a simple way to practice *Lectio Divina:*

1. Find a time and place when you can have a few quiet minutes to yourself.

2. Sit in a comfortable chair, but not a chair that encourages drowsiness. Ask the Holy Spirit to open your mind and heart to the words you are about to read.

3. Open your Bible to the verses you will be proclaiming as lector.

4. Begin reading the words, slowly.

5. When a particular word or phrase grabs your attention or touches your heart, pause and re-read until you have this word or phrase in your mind.

6. Close your eyes and repeat the word or words silently to yourself.

7. Gently allow the word or phrase to lead you into an awareness of God's loving presence in and all around you.

8. Rest quietly and calmly in God's loving presence.

9. When it seems natural to do so, open your eyes and continue reading.

10. Repeat the process until you have gone through the entire reading.

If you have the time and opportunity, you may want to go through this prayer phase more than once. By praying with the verses you will proclaim, you allow God's word that is deeper than the human words of Scripture to settle more and more into your heart. Then, when you stand before the assembly at Mass, you will proclaim the word of God as much from your heart as from the Lectionary's printed pages.

Another, even simpler, approach to prayer with the scriptures you will proclaim is to simply recall that you are in God's loving presence, then silently read a written prayer. Eventually you may memorize this prayer so you will not need to read it. Here is a traditional prayer suitable for this purpose:

Come, Holy Spirit, fill the hearts of your faithful, and enkindle in them the fire of your love. Send forth your Spirit and they shall be created; and you shall renew the face of the earth. O God, who instructs the hearts of your faithful by the light of your Holy Spirit, grant us by the same Holy Spirit to be truly wise and ever to rejoice in his consolation. Through Christ our Lord. Amen.

Here is a more contemporary prayer:

Lord Jesus, Word of God, come in your Holy Spirit with the boundless love of your Father who is my Father, too. Enlighten my mind that I may better understand your word in Scripture. Help me to be more deeply aware of your presence in my deepest center, that I may proclaim the word of God from a heart filled with your love. Unworthy as I am, by your saving grace be on my lips, that I may proclaim the word of God in a way that will touch the hearts of all. Amen.[7]

Either of these prayers is appropriate to use for the third and final part of your preparation process. You may also find it appropriate to pray one or both prayers just prior to the beginning of the Mass at which you will serve as lector.

Remember that this, or a similar, process of preparation is essential; it is not optional. If you approach the Lectionary "cold," with no preparation at all, you short-change the congregation gathered for Mass, spiritually speaking. You end up doing little more than reading aloud words from the pages of the Lectionary.

When you prepare well, you serve in spirit and in truth. When you prepare well, you proclaim the word of God not only with your lips but from your heart, which is the essence of the lector's ministry.

1. Raymond E. Brown, *The Critical Meaning of the Bible* (Mahwah, NJ: Paulist Press, 1981), 23.
2. As mentioned earlier, I particularly recommend the *Word and Worship Desk Calendar* or *Pocket Calendar* (Mahwah, NJ: Paulist Press, 1-800-218-1903).
3. *Living Faith: Daily Catholic Devotions.* 10300 Watson Rd., St. Louis, MO 63127. *My Daily Visitor: Readings and Reflections for Every Day.* Our Sunday Visitor, 200 Noll Plaza, Huntington, IN 46750.
4. Donald Senior, general editor, *The Catholic Study Bible* (New York: Oxford University Press, 1990).
5. *The Catholic Study Bible*, 239. The NAB translation leaves the "h" in "holy Spirit" in lower case to reflect the undeveloped character of trinitarian theology in the New Testament.
6. Among the other translations you may wish to have on hand, particularly valuable are *The New Revised Standard Version: Catholic Edition*; and *The New Jerusalem Bible*.
7. Prayer written by Mitch Finley. All rights reserved.

Chapter 6

THE LECTOR INTERPRETS
THE WORD

NOW FOR SOME PRACTICAL, "how to" tips. You will learn more about the actual "doing" of the lector's task from experience than you can from any book. Still, there are some practical guidelines that we can discuss here. When you practice with other lectors-in-training, your instructor can help you with specific advice and constructive criticism. Keep in mind that when an instructor points out ways to improve your lectoring style you should never take such criticism as an attempt to hurt your feelings or embarrass you. Rather, everyone — even seasoned lectors — can always improve, so welcome all constructive criticism as simply a chance to become a more effective lector.

In the Introduction to Part II we outlined the basic skills you need to proclaim the readings effectively. In this final chapter, our purpose is just as practical, but the underlying concern is both theological and pastoral. This may come as a surprise, but *the way you proclaim the reading(s) has an impact on how the entire eucharistic assembly hears and understands the word of God.*

Not to get ahead of ourselves, however, let me go back to the beginning of my own experience as a lector. About a year after I began serving as a lector in my parish, I began to think more deeply about what I was doing. I had learned about the importance of the basic skills, the need to speak up and speak clearly, read not too fast, not too slow, use the microphone correctly, and so forth. But my actual experience as a lector suggested that something more happens during those moments when I proclaim the word of God at Mass.

I recalled some of the ideas we considered earlier in this book. I remembered that the Scriptures are the product of a long and involved historical process, one that we need to take into account when we read the Bible under any circumstances. The Old Testament readings in the Lectionary are the result of a centuries-long process of reflection on, and *interpretation* of, the religious experience of ancient Israel. The readings from the letters and other non-Gospel New Testament documents are the result of human reflection on and *interpretation* of the faith experience of the primitive Church.

Specific issues and questions arose in the early Christian communities. St. Paul and the other authors of New Testament documents applied their own faith experience, and that of the wider faith community, to these specific issues and questions. In doing so it was necessary for Paul to interpret how the Christian life ought to be lived in various situations and circumstances. In this he took direction from both the Christian community's collective memory of Jesus and the Spirit of the risen Christ present and active then and there.

But there is one more step that must take place before you and I can read or hear the Scriptures. Scholars who are experts in biblical Hebrew, Greek, and other ancient languages, must translate the ancient manuscripts into English, Spanish, or whatever language modern readers need in order to read and understand the Bible. Part of the translation process is *interpretation.*

Often a team of translators must choose among several possible translations of a given passage, each of which will give a slightly different twist to the meaning of the words. For example, here is the *New Revised Standard Version's* (NRSV) translation of Romans 13:10: "Love does no wrong to a neighbor; therefore, love is the fulfilling of the law." And here is the same verse from the translation used in the Lectionary, the *New American Bible* (NAB): "Love does no evil to the neighbor; hence, love is the fulfillment of the law."

Notice the subtle differences between the two translations? "Love does no wrong" is not as strong and biting as "Love does no evil." The scholars responsible for these two translations had a "judgement call" to make. Each team of translators had the same Greek words to translate, but by a process of *interpretation* each team decided on a different word. The NAB translators decided on "evil," while the NRSV translators chose "wrong." Thus, each gave us a slightly different *interpretation* of the text.

Many considerations go into the final decision as to which option to select, but in the end it is necessary to make a decision about the use of a particular translation/interpretation of a Scriptural text. Of course, translators, too, carry out their task in communion with the Holy Spirit present and active here and now.

You see, therefore, that at every stage in the development of the Scriptures, processes of *interpretation* go on. The Scriptural excerpts in the Lectionary are the final product of a centuries-long process of interpretation — interpretation of an ongoing experience of a personal and communal faith relationship with God, and later with Jesus who lived and taught, died and became the risen Lord — and interpretation by translators of the ancient texts.

The process of interpretation does not end even with the translated biblical texts, however. Each person who reads the Bible does so from a unique set of life experiences and preconceptions, and with unique issues and/or questions in mind. Therefore, as we read the Scriptures we can't help but *interpret* what we read. Indeed, each local community tends to interpret the Scriptures. This is why it is so important for both individuals and local faith communities to always be open to the insights and guidance of Scripture scholars and, ultimately, to the Church as a whole when it comes to interpreting the Bible.

Look at some of the wilder interpretations of the Bible bandied about by tele-evangelists, street-corner preachers, and well-meaning sects. This is what happens when people interpret the Scriptures in isolation from the community of Scripture scholarship and from the faith community of the Church as a whole.

More to the point at hand, however, there is no way that a lector can step aside from this ongoing process of interpretation. Indeed, each lector is also, willy-nilly, an *interpreter of the Scriptures.* If we diagram, albeit in a simplified manner, the historical flow from the foundational experiences of ancient Israel, to Jesus of Nazareth, to the early Church, down through two thousand years of Christian faith, to you as a lector at St. Whoever Parish, our diagram might look like this:

Ancient Israel → Hebrew Scriptures (interpretation) → life, teachings, death and resurrection of Jesus → "oral tradition/stories of Jesus" (interpretation) → New Testament documents (interpretation) → translators (interpretation) → lector (interpretation).

By now you may wonder how, exactly, a lector can possibly be an interpreter of the Scriptures. Obviously, you are not doing what scholar-translators do, working with the ancient texts. All the same, whether you are conscious of it or not, when you proclaim the Scriptures you can't help but interpret them, as well. When you stand before the eucharistic assembly and read you give a personal and specific *interpretation* to the Scriptural word of God. It is impossible to be a neutral "mouthpiece."

By the tone of voice you use, by the emphasis you place on certain words and phrases, by the pauses you make and do not make, you interpret the Scriptures for the congregation. Indeed, the process of interpretation doesn't stop even there. Each member of the assembly, in turn, interprets the lector's interpretation for himself or herself. Ideally, of course, the homilist does some homework and interprets the readings in a way that has a significant impact on the congregation's understanding of the readings.

Let's look at an example. Suppose the second reading for the day is 1 Corinthians 15:20-27. In print we cannot express a tone of voice, but clearly your tone of voice is one way you say something about both yourself and the reading. If your voice is a low monotone, for example, you say to the congregation: "This reading is *borrring,* and so am I." If you use an inappropriately melodramatic tone of voice, you say to the congregation, "I'm an actor, and this reading is my script." If you use an even, well-modulated voice that makes no attempt to draw attention to itself, you say, "The word of God is what's important here, not me." This is the best way to let the word of God come through.

When it comes to emphasis, we can give an example in print using an actual reading from the Lectionary. Let's say the reading is Romans 13:8-10. As you read, you may interpret-by-emphasis something like this:

> Brothers and *sisters: Owe* nothing to anyone, *except* to love *one another;* for the one who *loves another* has *fulfilled* the law. The commandments, "You shall *not* commit adultery; you shall not *kill;* you shall *not* steal; you shall not *covet,"* and whatever other *commandment* there may be, are summed up in *this* saying, namely, "You shall love *your neighbor* as yourself." *Love* does *no* evil to the neighbor; hence, love *is* the *fulfillment* of the law.

Notice that the words in italics receive emphasis arbitrarily, based on one particular person's choice. Other words or phrases could just as easily receive emphasis. It's up to you, as lector, to decide which words or phrases you want to emphasize based on your understanding of the reading and how you want to present it to the congregation. By doing this, you *interpret* the reading in a particular way for the eucharistic assembly. This is one reason the preparation process we discussed in Chapter 5 is so important. By learning what you can about the reading, and about its meaning, and by taking some time for prayer related to the reading, you can decide which words and phrases are most appropriate to emphasize.

Sometimes one of the most difficult issues a lector must deal with is how familiar the entire congregation is with a given reading. Say the first reading is the creation account from Genesis, which everyone is familiar with to the point that anyone in the congregation could almost recite it from memory:

> In the beginning, when God created the heavens and the earth, the earth was a formless wasteland, and darkness covered the abyss, while a mighty wind swept over the waters. Then God said, "Let there be light," and there was light. God saw how good the light was. God then separated the light from the darkness. God called the light "day," and the darkness he called "night." Thus evening came, and morning followed — the first day (1:1-5).

The temptation with an overly familiar reading is to rush through it and read it with a tone of voice that says, "We have all heard this one countless times, so let's get it over with." The challenge to you, the lector, is to proclaim Scriptural texts the congregation knows well in such a way that they sound fresh and new. You can do this by learning, in advance, as much as you can about the reading, and then by proclaiming the reading in a way that gives it a lively interpretation. You want to use a tone of voice that says, "This is an amazing story." Instead of emphasizing the words and phrases everyone might expect you to emphasize, choose instead to place the emphasis on unexpected words and phrases. For example, emphasize "created" instead of "God;" inject just a tiny bit of drama into "darkness covered the abyss," and "a mighty wind swept over the waters."

By using subtle techniques such as these, you can help the congregation resist the inclination to think to itself, "I know this one like the back of my hand," and quickly slip into a semi-comatose state. By the interpretation you give the reading you can help people hear meanings they have never heard before.

Finally, it is critical that you keep in mind the literary style of a particular reading. Introductions and footnotes in *The Catholic Study Bible,* or your Bible commentary, explain about the literary style of each book in the Bible. Remember to take that into account as you prepare to do your reading. The creation story from Genesis is just that, a *story.* It's a story that carries divinely revealed truths, to be sure, but it's a story all the same. So read it like a story, not like you're reading from a newspaper.

If you have ever read a story to a child, learn something from that experience. You don't read a story to a child in a boring voice, you put some life into it. Obviously, you don't think of the congregation as a room full of children. All the same, the people there for Mass don't want to be bored by how you read. Put some life into your voice, and without getting silly about it, read like what you are reading is interesting, even fascinating. Because it is.

The letters of St. Paul, on the other hand, are letters, not stories. So read as you would if you were reading aloud to a friend a letter from a mutual friend. You need to be on your toes, however. Sometimes in his letters St. Paul quotes other literary styles. In the Letter to the Philippians, for example, Paul quotes from what is most likely an early Christian hymn in which believers sang of Jesus who, "though he was in the form of God, did not regard equality with God something to be grasped. Rather, he emptied himself, taking the form of a slave, coming in human likeness; and found human in appearance, he humbled himself, becoming obedient to death, even death on a cross" (2:6-8).

Even though you are working with a modern English translation of the words the early Christians sang, you can still sense a special rhythm in the words and phrases. As you get to these words Paul quotes, change your tone of voice a little and let a gentle rhythm affect the way you speak. If you merely keep reading along as if nothing is different, you miss an opportunity to make the reading come alive in a special way for the congregation.

Keep the various Scriptural literary styles in mind as you proclaim the word of God: The Psalms were originally sung, so even if the congregation does not sing the Responsorial Psalm keep the rhythm of the psalm in mind as you read it. The "Letter" to the Hebrews is not really a letter, it's more of a sermon or even a catechetical tract. The Book of Revelation isn't history or a scientific essay, it's more of a theological fantasy — one that carries divine truths, to be sure, but a theological fantasy all the same. And so forth.

Keep the literary style of the Scriptural texts you read from in mind, and let that style affect the way you carry out your ministry as a lector. Let it make a difference in how you use your voice, in the words and phrases you emphasize, in the rhythm with which you read, and in the way you pause between words, phrases, and sentences.

Afterword
CARRY THE WORD OF GOD WITH YOU

> Indeed, the word of God is living and effective, sharper than any two-edged sword, penetrating even between soul and spirit, joints and marrow, and able to discern reflections and thoughts of the heart.
>
> — HEBREWS 4:12

AS A LECTOR, you are called to have a particular devotion to the Scriptures. But there is nothing sentimental or maudlin about this devotion, and there is nothing simple-minded about it. A lector is the last one in the world who should be content with a fundamentalist or even a quasi-fundamentalist understanding of the Scriptures. A lector is also the last one who should think that he or she can be nothing but a neutral "mouthpiece" for the word of God. Rather, a lector is called to cultivate an active love for the Scriptures, and be a continuing student of — not an expert on — the Scriptures. In this way, when you stand before the eucharistic assembly to proclaim the word of God it will come from your heart and mind more than from your lips.

It's a shame that Catholics are not known for their devotion to the Scriptures. After all, it was the

Church, in its earliest centuries, that embraced the Hebrew Scriptures and gave birth to the New Testament. It was St. Jerome (c. 340-420), the greatest Bible scholar of the early Church who said, "To be ignorant of the Scriptures is not to know Christ." The widespread lack of familiarity with the Scriptures among Catholics is, therefore, most unfortunate. This situation presents an opportunity, however. Lectors have the opportunity to become leaders in their parishes when it comes to giving the Scriptures a more prominent place in Catholic life.

As a lector, you are called not merely to stand up and read aloud from the Lectionary every few weeks or so, when your turn rolls around again. Rather, you are called to live with the word of God which is God's constant revelation of Himself or Herself in time and space. And one of the most fundamental ways to cultivate sensitivity to God's word is through intimacy with the Scriptures which both carry God's word and make you more receptive to God's word as it enters the world in other ways, too. These other ways include official Church teachings, of course, but they also include everyday events both ordinary and extraordinary. If you are tuned to it by love for and familiarity with the Scriptures, you can encounter the word of God in a newspaper, in a stranger, in a child, in a movie, in a song, and in endless other ways.

As a lector, you are called to carry God's word with you in your heart every day. As a lector, you are called to speak God's word not just when you proclaim that word from the Lectionary during Mass. You are called to speak God's word in your everyday life, in your interactions with other people, in your work and in your leisure activities. You are called, as a lector, to *become* a "word of God" in your little corner of the world.

Is this not true for all Christians? Of course it is. But as a lector you are called to become a leader-by-example. So: "Let the word of Christ dwell in you richly. . ." (Colossians 3:16).

Not to get too abstract, however, there is one practical point that all lectors should never forget. Here it is: If you can't be there when you are scheduled to serve as lector, *it's your responsibility to find a replacement.*

Amen.

Postscript

IN CASE YOU WONDER if there is a patron saint for lectors, you're in luck. There are, in fact, two patron saints. Both lived in the fourth century and died for their faith. The first is St. Pollio, the second St. Sabas.[1]

St. Pollio was a lector in the Christian community of Cybalae, Lower Pannonia, on the Danube, in what later became Mikanovici, Yugoslavia. Pollio became leader of the community after Bishop Eusebius was martyred. In 304, Pollio ignored the edicts of the Roman emperor, Diocletian, and then refused to offer sacrifice to pagan gods. Soon thereafter, he was condemned to death and burned at the stake. His feast day is April 28.

St. Sabas was a Goth who converted to Christianity as a youth and became a lector in Targoviste, Romania. After surviving several persecutions under the pagan Goths, in 372 Sabas was captured by some Gothic soldiers who demanded that he offer sacrifice to idols. Sabas was tortured horribly along with several other Christians, then finally drowned in the Mussovo River, near Targoviste. Some fifty others were put to death with him. St. Sabbas' feast day is April 12.

Sts. Pollio and Sabas, pray for us.

---

1. The information on these two saints comes from Matthew Bunson, et al., *Our Sunday Visitor's Encyclopedia of Saints* (Huntington, IN: Our Sunday Visitor Publishing Division, 1998), and from John J. Delaney, *Dictionary of Saints* (New York: Doubleday & Co., 1980).

Recommended Reading

Raymond E. Brown, S.S., *The Critical Meaning of the Bible* (Mahwah, NJ: Paulist Press, 1981).

Raymond E. Brown, S.S., *An Introduction to the New Testament* (New York: Doubleday & Co., 1997).

Raymond E. Brown, S.S., *Responses to 101 Questions on the Bible* (Mahwah, NJ: Paulist Press, 1990).

Raymond E. Brown, S.S., et al., general editors, *The New Jerome Biblical Commentary* (Englewood Cliffs, NJ: Prentice Hall, Inc., 1990).

Joseph M. Champlin, *The Mystery and Meaning of the Mass* (New York: The Crossroad Publishing Co., 1999).

Austin Flannery, O.P., general editor, "Dogmatic Constitution on Divine Revelation," in *Vatican Council II: The Conciliar and Post Conciliar Documents,* New Revised Edition (Northport, NY: Costello Publishing Co., 1992).

Luke Timothy Johnson, *The Real Jesus: The Misguided Quest for the Historical Jesus and the Truth of the Traditional Gospels* (San Francisco: HarperSan Francisco, 1996).

John L. McKenzie, *Dictionary of the Bible* (New York: Macmillan Publishing Co., 1965).

Bruce M. Metzger and Michael D. Coogan, editors, *The Oxford Companion to the Bible* (New York: Oxford University Press, 1993).

Additional Titles Published by Resurrection Press, a Catholic Book Publishing Imprint

A Rachel Rosary *Larry Kupferman*	$4.50
Blessings All Around *Dolores Leckey*	$8.95
Catholic Is Wonderful *Mitch Finley*	$4.95
Discernment *Chris Aridas*	$8.95
Edge of Greatness *Joni Woelfel*	$9.95
Growing through the Stress of Ministry *Muto/van Kaam*	$7.95
Grace Notes *Lorraine Murray*	$9.95
Healing through the Mass *Robert DeGrandis, SSJ*	$9.95
Our Grounds for Hope *Fulton J. Sheen*	$7.95
The Healing Rosary *Mike D.*	$5.95
Healing the Wounds of Emotional Abuse *Nancy deFlon*	$6.95
Heart Peace *Adolfo Quezada*	$9.95
Hold Fast to Hope *Linda Rooney*	$6.95
Life, Love and Laughter *Jim Vlaun*	$7.95
The Joy of Being an Altar Server *Joseph Champlin*	$5.95
The Joy of Being a Bereavement Minister *Nancy Stout*	$5.95
The Joy of Being a Catechist *Gloria Durka*	$4.95
The Joy of Being a Eucharistic Minister *Mitch Finley*	$5.95
The Joy of Being a Lector *Mitch Finley*	$5.95
The Joy of Being an Usher *Gretchen Hailer, RSHM*	$5.95
The Joy of Marriage Preparation *McDonough/Marinelli*	$5.95
The Joy of Music Ministry *J.M. Talbot*	$6.95
The Joy of Praying the Rosary *James McNamara*	$5.95
The Joy of Teaching *Joanmarie Smith*	$5.95
Lessons for Living from the 23rd Psalm *Victor M. Parachin*	$6.95
Lights in the Darkness *Ave Clark, O.P.*	$8.95
Loving Yourself for God's Sake *Adolfo Quezada*	$5.95
Magnetized by God *Robert E. Lauder*	$8.95
Mercy Flows *Rod Damico*	$9.95
Mother Teresa *Eugene Palumbo, S.D.B.*	$5.95
Mourning Sickness *Keith Smith*	$8.95
The Power of One *Jim Lisante*	$9.95
Praying the Lord's Prayer with Mary *Muto/vanKaam*	$8.95
5-Minute Miracles *Linda Schubert*	$4.95
Sabbath Moments *Adolfo Quezada*	$6.95
Season of New Beginnings *Mitch Finley*	$4.95
Sometimes I Haven't Got a Prayer *Mary Sherry*	$8.95
The Spiritual Spa *Mary Sherry*	$9.95
St. Katharine Drexel *Daniel McSheffery*	$12.95
What He Did for Love *Francis X. Gaeta*	$5.95
Woman Soul *Pat Duffy, OP*	$7.95
You Are My Beloved *Mitch Finley*	$10.95

For a free catalog call 1-800-892-6657
www.catholicbookpublishing.com